A Backwards Glance

"Events in Aylsham's past"

Published by the Aylsham Local History Society

A Backwards Glance

Acknowledgements

Much of the source material, photographs and the illustration used on the cover of this publication form part of the collection in the Aylsham Archives. We would like to thank the Aylsham Town Council for allowing us to use them.

Aylsham Local History Society
Editorial Committee:

Geoffrey Gale, Chairman
Valerie Belton
Julian Eve
Tom Mollard

ISBN 0-9521564-6-6

A Backwards Glance

"Events in Aylsham's past"

Contents

A Backwards Glance

*'Out of monuments, names, words, proverbs, traditions, private records and evidences,
fragments of stories, passages of books, and the like, we do save and recover
somewhat from the deluge of time.'*

This quotation by Mr. R. W. Ketton Cremer in his 'Norfolk Assembly' came to mind, when I was asked to write an introduction for this modest collection of papers. They record some part of the work which members of the Society have undertaken during the past ten years. They cover in particular the work we have more recently undertaken in our examination of the local archives which are held in the Town Hall and what we have felt interesting enough to recover 'from the deluge of time'.

Our Local History Society was founded in 1984. It grew out of a series of WEA classes given by Mr. J. C. Barringer, then Senior Tutor of the Cambridge Extra Mural Board in Norfolk. It is my recollection that these classes were entitled 'A History of Aylsham'; certainly I went along to them expecting to hear the history of Aylsham unfold before me, but my expectations were not fulfilled. Almost immediately I found myself doing the 'research' - reading documents such as 'manor court rolls' and 'terriers', delving actively into the past in a way I had never envisaged and, thanks to Christopher Barringer's enthusiasm, getting thoroughly hooked on to the whole process of discovering history for myself.

After two years these classes ended and some of us decided to form a society to continue our interest in local history. Under the chairmanship of the Rev. Jack Vyse the Aylsham Local History Society came into being. Gradually a programme of public lectures was arranged with help from the Centre of East Anglian Studies and others, and a small research group took on what was quite a daunting task - the translation of the Aylsham Rental of c.1624, published as 'Aylsham in the Seventeenth Century' in 1989. Finding that as students we were ill equipped for the study of early documents, the next development was to initiate classes in which we were helped with palaeography by Mrs. Elizabeth Rutledge and enabled to embark on further studies which in turn have led to further publications: - 'Aylsham in 1821' published in 1989, contains the details of the first census returns, and the booklet on Millgate was published in 1993. These publications were additional to the regular quarterly production of the Society's Journal & Newsletter which had been started in 1985 by Tom Mollard and continues to be enjoyed by members and non-members both here in Aylsham and by those who have moved away. As we have become established, the range of our activities has increased: in addition to a regular winter/spring series of lectures we have found time for day-schools on vernacular architecture, yearly "mystery history" tours, a New Year Party which has become a traditional January event, and regular daylong coach trips to places of historical interest. We have made connections with other like minded organisations, such as the Norfolk Archaeological and Historical Research Group and the Federation of Norfolk Historical and Archaeological Organisations, and some of us are Associate members of the Centre of East Anglian Studies. This led to our participation in events such as the Norfolk Nonconformist Chapel Study of 1988-1993, and the history fairs held at Gressenhall Museum and Blickling Park. A small group of us have recently developed an interest in Oral History and have set about recording the memories of our older citizens. And finally, in the Town Hall last July, we put together an exhibition celebrating the activities of our first ten years.

Now in 1995 we are turning our attention to more publications. In this booklet we aim to record what we put on display on that July weekend. It is a collection of articles summarising the exhibits, so that the information which we had put together in photographs, drawings and written panels is recorded in more permanent form.

We will also have for sale by subscription shortly a reproduction of the 1839 Wright's Map of Aylsham and its accompanying schedules, as well as an account of the Poor Law in Aylsham by Julian Eve. Meantime our 'Archives' group continues to meet and pore over papers and records from our archives and other documents which come our way, and we look forward to our next ten years of discovery.

Jane Nolan
Chairman, Aylsham Local History Society

A Time Chart of Aylsham

Date	National events	Aylsham events
43 - 410	Romans	
400		
410 - 1066	Anglo Saxons	
500		Foundation of Aegel's homestead C500 - 600
800	Danish Invasions Mid C8 - C10	
880		Danish colonisation of East Anglia
900		
1000		
1066 - 1154	Normans	
1075		Aylsham a Royal manor. Church in existence
1086		Domesday Book. Two mills in Aylsham
1087		William II gave patronage of St Michael's Church to Battle Abbey, between 1087 - 1100
1100		
1154 - 1485	Plantagenets	
1199		Richard I gave part of the capital manor of Aylsham to the Abbey of Bury St. Edmunds (Sexton's Manor) King John gave another part of the capital manor of Aylsham to Hugh de Boves (Bolwick Manor)
1200		
1250		Aylsham developing textile industry, Aylsham Web (linen) and later Worstead (woollen) weaving
1300		
1337 - 1453	Hundred Years' War	
1372		Edward III gave the remainder of the Capital manor of Aylsham to his son. John of Gaunt, as tenant. (Aylsham Lancaster)
1380		Parish Church rebuilt
1390		Use of the Buttlands for archery practice
1400		Sir Thomas Erpingham tenant of Aylsham Lancaster Manor
1455 - 1485	Wars of the Roses	
1485 - 1603	Tudors	
1500		
1530		Robert Jannys Mayor of Norwich founded Aylsham Grammar School
1536 - 1540	Dissolution of the monasteries	
1540		The Dean and Chapter of Canterbury became patrons of St Michael's Church. The Manor of Aylsham Sexton became the Manor of Aylsham Wood
1550		Manor House Cromer Road built 1550 (extended by Bishop Jegon 1611)
1600		
1603 - 1714	The Stuarts	
1634		Manor of Aylsham Lancaster sold to Sir John Hobart
1640		Cressy's Charity houses for the poor established in the 1640's
1642 - 1649	The Civil War	

1660	Restoration	
1700		
1714 - 1837	The Hanoverians	
1723		First mention of Parish Fire Engine
1750		
1756 - 1763	Seven Years' War	
1770	The Industrial Revolution	
1773	Boston Tea Party	
1775 - 1783	The American War of Independence.	
1776		Aylsham Workhouse built
1779		Opening of Aylsham Navigation
		Birth of Joseph Clover, Artist
1789	The French Revolution	
1790		Baptist Church opening
1791 - 1792	Thomas Paine, "Rights of Man"	
1793 - 1815	The French Wars	
1794		Opening of Norwich to Aylsham Turnpike
1800		
1811		Aylsham to Cromer Turnpike
1818		Humphry Repton died
1825		
1834		Poor Law Amendment Act established Aylsham Union in 1836
1837	Accession of Queen Victoria	
1838		Tithe Award
1839		Wright's Map of Aylsham
1849		Opening of the Aylsham Workhouse now Saint Michael's Hospital
1850		Opening of Aylsham Gas Works
1851	The Great Exhibition	
1854 - 1856	The Crimean War	
1857		Opening of the Aylsham Town Hall, originally as a Corn Exchange
1861 - 1865	American Civil War	
1871		Aylsham to Cromer tramway proposed
1875		
1880		Great Eastern Railway line opened between Aylsham and Norwich
1894		Aylsham Parish Council set up
1897	Queen Victoria's Diamond Jubilee	
1899 - 1902	Boer War	
1900		
1912		Aylsham Flood
1914 - 1918	First World War	
1925		
1929		Electricity reached Aylsham
1938		Piped supply of water in Aylsham
1939 - 1945	Second World War	
1940		Aylsham Lancaster taken over by National Trust
1950		
1951	1951 Exhibition	Great Eastern Railway Line closed in Aylsham
1952	Accession of Elizabeth II	
1956		Cottage Hospital opened
1975		
1981		The building of the Aylsham By-Pass
1984		Formation of Aylsham Local History Society
1990		The narrow gauge Bure Valley Railway opened
1993		Aylsham Flood

The Poor Relief in Aylsham 1700 - 1836

From Tudor times up until the passing of the Poor Law Amendment Act in 1834 every parish was responsible for its own poor. A Poor Rate was levied compulsorily on every householder in the parish according to the value of his property, to be used in various ways to relieve the poor. Two (or more) Overseers of the Poor were appointed at the Easter Vestry Meeting each year to collect the rate and distribute the money for the benefit of the poor. The Overseers served for a year and then handed over the balance of the money to their successors. Each usually served for six months. Careful accounts had to be kept and these had to be approved by the local magistrates each year. At Aylsham the surviving account books, and there are more than 40 of them, date from 1674 and continue right up to the formation of the Aylsham Poor Law Union in 1836.

In 1993 some members of the archive group of the Aylsham Local History Society decided to analyse these accounts. It shows the overseers' annual disbursement on the poor from 1750 to 1834. The population of Aylsham and a few major events are also recorded.

Aylsham overseers' disbursement on poor relief 1750-1834

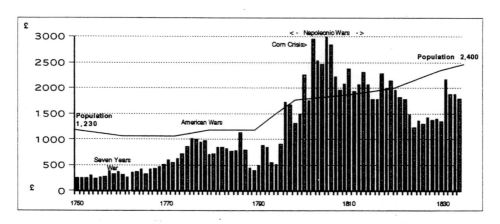

Before 1750 the amount rate payers had to find was rarely more than £250 in any one year, about two shillings in the pound, and this was well within their means. A poor or failed harvest always led to an increase in distress as did a hard winter or local epidemic illness. There were poor harvests in 1733, 1741 when smallpox was also rife, and in 1756. The winter of 1767 was the coldest of the century and followed a poor harvest the previous year in which there had been food riots in Norwich.

During the American Wars (1775-1782), trade was disrupted and this caused a marked increase in unemployment and the cost of poor relief increased to £1,000. Aylsham responded by building a workhouse as a house of industry where the able-bodied paupers could earn something towards paying for their keep. Poor harvests, and smallpox outbreaks in Norfolk added to the troubles of the poor during the 1770s and 1780s. There was smallpox in Aylsham in 1774 and again in 1783-4. The real crisis came with the onset of the French Revolutionary and Napoleonic Wars (1793-1802 & 1803-1815) when the cost of corn reached famine prices. Within a few years the amount disbursed annually on poor relief went from £500 to £3,000. Aylsham was particularly badly hit. In 1803 the per capita expenditure on poor relief was: - Aylsham, £1 12s 2d. Norfolk, 12s 5d. England & Wales, 8s 11d. The table below shows how desperate things became for agricultural labourers in Norfolk.

Year	Average agricultural wage	Equivalent number of loaves of bread
1760	- 5s a week	28 loaves
1785	- 8s	16 loaves
1792	- 9s	15 loaves
1803	- 10s	12 loaves
1812	- 9s	9 loaves
1817	- 9s	7 loaves

After the Napoleonic War was over rate payers soon started to complain and this eventually led to the Poor Law Amendment Act of 1834. The Aylsham Union of 46 parishes was formed in 1836 and costs to the parish were reduced.

Although every parish was responsible for its own poor there was often doubt as to who was a true settled inhabitant and entitled to poor relief. The Settlement Act of 1662 established strict rules with regard to settlement so that anyone in need would know where to turn; but the Act also stated that strangers could be removed back to their place of settlement within 40 days if they were thought likely to become a charge on the parish. Some parishes became almost "closed" parishes where the local landholder made sure strangers were not employed for fear of them later becoming a charge on the parish. This made it difficult for the unemployed to seek work outside their own parish. Where there was doubt the pauper could be brought before the magistrates who decided the pauper's place of settlement.

In 1697 the Act of Settlement was modified and church wardens and overseers were permitted to supply a certificate to those wishing to leave their parish acknowledging the parish's liability for poor relief should they become destitute while living in another parish. Furthermore, certificate holders could not be removed until they actually became chargeable. Eventually, in 1795, this right was extended to all migrants and from then on the English labourer was able to remain in whatever parish he chose as long as he remained solvent.

The acknowledgement certificates that new entrants to a parish brought with them were always preserved by the overseers so that the stranger's place of settlement was known.

The upper chart was constructed by using the 150 acknowledgement certificates kept by the Aylsham overseer between 1700 and 1790 and shows how far people came in search of work. They hailed from 80 different parishes but most of them were within walking distance.

The poor in their search for work in Aylsham

- ■ Under 10 miles
- ▨ 10 to 20 miles
- ▨ From Norwich
- ▨ Over 20 miles

In spite of the strict settlement laws there was a fair amount of movement in search of work, and by examining the extant Removal Orders, issued to families by the magistrates, to move in or out of Aylsham, we can get some idea of the numbers. The lower graph covers the years 1700 to 1815 and represents 169 removal orders involving some 500 people if the wives and families are included.

Removal orders issued by the Magistrates to Aylsham paupers 1700-1815

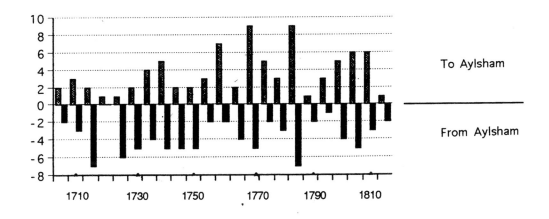

To Aylsham

From Aylsham

Hungate Street

Hungate Street, like many other country neighbourhoods, is lined with houses of different styles and ages. Some of its history is written on its face, but more is hidden by external changes or has been destroyed outright.

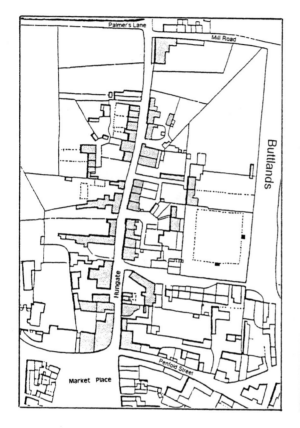

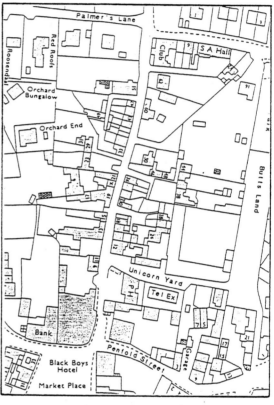

Hungate Street 1700–1800   Hungate Street 1970

As we look from the north, the Unicorn public house dominates. It is a timber-framed building of the fourteenth or fifteenth century, but it has long been completely rendered outside. On the left is the bulk of Norfolk House, which was given its present shape in the late eighteenth century. Most houses at this end of the street show gentrification of the eighteenth century: they are of brick, some with tall windows (nos. 12, 14, 15), three have door-cases (nos. 12, 14, 15), some have dentillation under the eaves (nos. 15, 30, 32, 34). Half of no. 18 is timber-framed, with a brick house built on to it. Another of this type (with dentillation) is no. 28 in a yard to the west. No.22 beside it, much extended, was built in 1821 by C.R. Wade, a watchmaker. Returning to the street, the viewer sees a grand eighteenth-century house (no. 64) with a portico in the distance. Most of the rest is very small cottages and an ugly gap. The remains of another yard to the west contains the home of the first Baptist minister in Aylsham (1817-48), and a thatched house that was once a row of four cottages.

Besides the evidence of our eyes, there are documents attesting the history of some buildings. The best of these is a rental of the manor of Aylsham Lancaster, compiled not before 1624 (henceforth Rental*). Records of the manor court are also useful: the court rolls which in the seventeenth century were succeeded by court books (henceforth CB). In the Rental at least twelve occupied premises are recorded in Hungate Street. A few on the east side can be identified. The very large house (10 bays) owned by Thomas Munday and called Hobbes must be Norfolk House, still referred to by his name in CB 1739 where its identity is clear. There are a few internal signs of great antiquity in this house; the name Hobbes first occurs in a court roll of 1464. The house does not face the street, but looks north. By 1624 it was already divided into four tenements. Although Thomas Munday was recently dead when the Rental was compiled, his son John did not return to claim the house until 1640. When it is next mentioned (CB 1739), the house appears to be in poor condition: a cellar is listed, with rooms over it; there is 'liberty to repair on the south part of the chimney', and allowance is made for general repairs. John Repton acquired the house in 1764, and his son Humphry sold it to John Warnes of Bolwick in 1797, who probably gave it its present shape.

The Rental lists four houses belonging wholly or in part to James Gogle in Hungate Street. One lay N.E. of Norfolk House, had an entrance to the street, a garden and the right to draw water. This property became the bowling-green of the Dog Inn, but is still 'formerly Gogles' in CB 1797.

The long low house (no. 17-19) appears to be seventeenth-century but its history has not been traced beyond CB 1720, when it was acquired by Henry Wymark under the name of The Half Moon. Soon after 1748 a bakery was set up, and a bakery it remained until the late Mr Postle retired c.1950.

No. 21 came into the possession of the owner of the Half Moon in 1777. Here the property is called Pecks; it is first so named in CB 1720, when the heirs of John Leverington claimed their inheritance some years after his death. It would seem to be the 'cottage' surrendered by Edward Peck (CB 1555). It has a brick-lined cellar which appears to be several centuries old. The position of the house on the east side of the street is further confirmed by certain specifications in CB 1720: the tenant is to have free access to Chapman's Lane, a venella running behind the houses through gardens and orchards to the market place.

One more property, not now identifiable, can be placed on the eastern side of the street. In September 1611 Firmin Lawes (d. 1615) surrendered a messuage in Hungate Street 'commonly called the old gaole' to Christopher Reve and Thomas Akers; together with a parcel of its cultivated land fundus which was divided by a wall from another section of the property. From the Rental we learn that Thomas Lawes, son and heir of Firmin Lawes, at the same time received a parcel of fundus with a barn and garden (1 rood in all) in Hungate Street, which lay 'outside the eastern wall dividing the said barn &c'. This must surely be a part of Firmin's property which he made over to his son when he sold the house. The piece of land with its barn is still traceable in CB entries of 1734 and 1735. I cannot place it, but the 'eastern wall' would most naturally refer to a boundary wall behind a house on the east side of the street. The old gaol vanishes in 1614, on the second transfer. Perhaps it was pulled down.

The half-timbered house no.35 belonged to the manor of Aylsham Vicarage. This appears to be the cottage bought by John Proudfoot (carpenter and father of carpenters) in 1822. No. 47 incorporates a sixteenth-century cottage, also within the manor of Aylsham Vicarage. This adds two more houses to the dozen of the Rental.

On the west side, much physical evidence has been removed this century. The Swan public house which stood on the corner of Mill Road was a seventeenth-century house, judging by its photographs. A house of similar age stood at the roadside near no. 46. Two houses that can be documented lay at this end of the street. Both belonged to Simon Leverington. The smaller one, of 3 bays, was bought in 1618 and seems to correspond to a CB entry of 1729. The other apparently covered the present surgery, and much more. It was bought in 1608, had 10 bays, 'a fair parlour', a large barn, a small barn and gardens. This property appears in the will of Simon Leverington, dated 1652. He leaves 'the houses in my yards now occupied by Laurence Burr, with that part of the yard from the Buttland wall to my little barn door' to his widowed daughter. Everything else (and the reversion of this bequest) went to his only son Matthew. The John Leverington who died 1719-20 in possession of Peck's was probably related to Simon, who had at least one brother in Norwich.

It appears that the street was fairly built up by 1624, and that little farmland existed at the town end. The Rental locates some 19 acres of unbuilt land in Hungate. It is safe to assume that most of this lay south of what is now Mill Road. Still, there were 2 acres alongside Hobbes (bought 1593) and Thomas Smith (site unknown) had held a house and two cottages with 2 acres attached since 1575. Householders with a barn on the premises were: Thomas Munday, Thomas Smith, Margaret Chosell and Simon Leverington (2). The open country was not far away, and Hungate Street was a desirable refuge from it.

Published by Aylsham Local History Society as Aylsham in the Seventeenth Century, 1988

The Bure Navigation 1779 - 1912

This account concerns the physical features of the navigation which can be found along its course. There is now no use of the water by boats and there is only riverbank access from Coltishall up to Mayton Bridge, marked on the early O.S. maps as a tow-path. This was not a canal but a river navigation and only used by wherries which could be sailed or quanted when there was no wind so that a tow-path was not needed. Access to the waterway is therefore restricted and it is unknown to most apart from quick glimpses from the few bridges (five originally) which really need the driver's eyes on the road.

It would seem that the navigation was over ambitious and underfunded with the moving about of parts of a river involving considerable amounts of excavation by manpower (the fore-runners of the Navvies) with primitive equipment, Archemedian screws, horses and carts, wheel-barrows, etc., it is not surprising that they ran out of money and contractors had second thoughts. More information on this side of the concern lies in the Account Books and other material lodged in the Archives at Aylsham Town Hall.

The River Bure is slightly tidal as far as Horstead and wherries trading on the Broads found their way above this point blocked by a series of four mills, mostly dating back to Domesday or earlier. There is some evidence that the Roman pottery industry based at Brampton used water transport to distribute Brampton ware up and down the east coast but the river may have been deeper in those days. The first lock (G.R. 267194) was built at Horstead on a cut off channel avoiding the mill. This lock had a rise of 5 ft which maintained the level as far as Buxton. A short distance above Horstead Church on the east side of the river (G.R. 260200) a footbridge crosses a small stream issuing out of old marl workings. This was a much smaller version of what is now known as Little Switzerland (G.R. 275174) further down the river. The method used was to excavate down to the water level and to load the marl directly into lighters or wherries. As the cutting progressed into the hillside the workings became deeper. There, above Horstead, forward progress was blocked by the Horstead to Buxton road and the cutting turned round on itself ending in a short spiral now overgrown with trees. Coltishall on the other side of the river had several channels leading to pits and limekilns. A very large and well preserved kiln can be seen at the back of the Railway Inn. It is of the unusual Norfolk type and very impressive (G.R. 268203).

A little over half way to Buxton is Mayton bridge (G.R. 250216). There the problem concerned the 15th Century bridge of two pointed arches far too restricted to take wherries. A long straight new channel was cut and a new bridge of unusual design was built. The bridge as it is today has been lowered but two circular openings in the piers still remain and must have been intended to relieve flood water.

Just before Buxton the railway crosses on a bend of the river on an ugly metal bridge. The wherrymen said that this had been done deliberately to make sailing awkward for them (G.R. 238224).

Buxton Mill (G.R. 237228) stands firmly across the river. There, Biedermann, who laid out the navigation, shows an 11ft rise by means of two locks. But a single lock was built here which was cleared away when the road was remade in the 1930s. It must have been a very difficult place with the lock very close to the mill and with some kind of bridge that would open. The channel leading to the lock site still exists as does another one that leads to what may have been a wharf below a sluice. Mr Pepper, the miller here, became a navigation commissioner, owned wherries and managed to get his overshot waterwheel channel constructed as part of the navigation. This left the river just above Oxnead Mill and made its way to holding ponds near the mill - the channel, now dry, can be followed winding across the fields. The reach above Buxton Mill extends as far as Oxnead mainly as a large bend crossed at one point by a Roman road. At Oxnead Mill the lock is now a sluice off the wide mill pond-like part of the river. Just above this storage area there is a typical narrow hump-backed canal bridge. Brick built of a single arch it has carried traffic for over 200 years but is unloved by present day motorists. The rise at Oxnead was 5½ ft though Biedermann does not show this lock on his plan (G.R. 227239).

From Oxnead the level is maintained to Burgh. The early O.S. maps show a lime kiln by the waterway upstream from Oxnead Bridge and there is still a farm called Lime Kiln Farm on the Brampton to Tuttington road (G.R. 226243). It would seem that chalky marl was quarried from just below the road and probably carried by water in a narrow channel to the kiln. The river here flows through wide water-meadows with Brampton, the site of the small Roman industrial town on higher ground to the west.

At Burgh the navigation made great changes to the course of the river and it was these works which probably led to the loss of capital that caused much financial trouble and the decamping of the contractor - John Smith. Originally the river swung to the east to go round to the lower side of Burgh Mill (G.R. 223252). This still carries water from the tailrace. The navigation was put on an embankment which leads off from just above the mill. Burgh lock, brick built from locally fired bricks and now a sluice, stands at the outer end of the embankment with a rise of 5½ ft. The whole river is embanked from above the mill to the Church. Some original wooden boarding and tie rods can still be found in the bankside. The stretch from the Church, under Burgh bridge, and upstream from the bridge is all man-made. Originally the river swung away from the Church towards the farm (Brampton Hall)(G.R. 218247) where the footbridge over the Mermaid stream now is, then along the present course of the stream almost to the present day railway bridge. Before these alterations the road from Aylsham to Burgh must have crossed the old river several hundred yards nearer Aylsham. Because of these changes there were problems with bringing in the Mermaid stream to join the main river and with draining the low-lying fields - a maze of ditches, some passing under others by culverts, resulted.

About a mile above Burgh Bridge Biedermann decided to leave the course of the river (G.R. 212264) and dig a channel alongside the river across the low-lying fields up to Aylsham. This may have been because the river was too winding and too shallow. On this first long straight channel there are the remains of Wolsey Bridge - demanded by a Mr Wolsey as access to land that had become an island. Further up are the remains of Aylsham Lock (G.R. 210273), (or Burgh Hall Lock 51½ft) which controlled the level of the water at Aylsham Staithe and allowed access to the rear of Aylsham Mill. This lock was strangely remote and is now crumbling away amongst trees rooted in the brickwork.

The glimpse of the river and navigation seen from the by-pass bridge is disappointing. Both appear to be little more than overgrown channels and it has been said that major alterations were made when the by-pass was built - certainly the River Bure is not seen at its broad best (G.R. 206276).

And so into 'industrial Aylsham'. "The Key" as originally drawn on the plan was oval in shape but eventually became a complex of basins and short arms which, in its heyday, was a busy place for both goods and passengers and much to the benefit of the town. Wherries were built here and families connected with the navigation lived in Millgate where there were also wherrymen's public houses (G.R. 198276).

All this ended in 1912 when the declining trade affected by the railways was brought to a close by a disastrous flood which swept away locks and river banks. It took many years, mainly because of the First World War, to wind up the affairs. Not until 1928 did the Navigation of 1779 cease to exist as such. Meanwhile the river flows on through the quiet countryside.

These notes are a condensation of a large display on a scale of 25 inches to 1 mile which was part of the Celebration Exhibition held in July 1994.

The following Ordnance Survey sheets will help in locating features mentioned.

Landranger Sheet 133 North East Norfolk (1:50,000)
2½ inches to 1 mile Sheet TG22/32 Norfolk Broads, North has most of the navigation on it.
TG02/12 (Pathfinder 861) Aylsham and Foulsham and
TG21/31 (Pathfinder 883) Norwich North and Wroxham complete the coverage.

Faden's map of Norfolk published some eighteen years after the opening of the Navigation is remarkably accurate being a forerunner of the Ordnance Survey. He has indicated a lock where the canal section left the River Bure above Burgh; a lock which did not exist. There are several lime kilns, brick kilns and other indications of industry connected with the waterway, most of which have now vanished.

Aylsham at Prayer

The aim of this study is to show the development of the religious life of the people of Aylsham over the centuries as revealed by church records and other documents and by buildings past and present.

The oldest church is of course the Parish Church, dedicated to St. Michael and All Angels and built on the site of an earlier church. In 1372, John of Gaunt, Duke of Lancaster, became the Lord of the Manor of Aylsham Lancaster and he is associated with the building of the church. The Reformation in the sixteenth century brought changes including the closing of the monasteries and alterations in the form of worship. The seventeenth century in its turn brought the Civil War, the Interregnum under Cromwell, and the Restoration of the Monarchy and the Church of England in 1660. In 1689 the Toleration Act allowed Dissenters (but not Roman Catholics or Unitarians) freedom of worship, but their premises had to be licensed by the bishop. Such worshipping congregations met at first in cottages, private houses, sheds and work places. Gradually, purpose built meeting houses or chapels began to appear. In 1829 the Roman Catholic Emancipation Act was passed.

Dissent in Aylsham

So far we have found no evidence for the existence of dissenting congregations in the town until late into the 18th century. From 1789 onwards, there appears to have been considerable activity amongst Baptists, Methodists, Independents and Swedenborgians, much of it centring round the first purpose built meeting house, the present Emmanuel Church in White Hart Street, known until recently as the Baptist Church.

The first references in the Dissenting Meeting Houses Register are as follows:
On the 27 June 1789 it was certified by Richard Jex of Aylsham, farmer.......that a certain house and building, hired by him of, and belonging to, Mr. William Rackham of Ripton (? Rippon) Hall in the said county, gentleman, situate in the said town of Aylsham, formerly used as a schoolroom, of late a combers shop is set apart for the exercise of religious worship of Almighty God by protestant dissenters.

Four months later the same Richard Jex certifies that a certain chapel or building newly erected by him ....*is set apart as a place of religious worship by protestant dissenters called Methodists.*

Baptists and Methodists differ over the early history of the building - ie who owned it and who used it. (See below for separate accounts under Baptist and Methodist headings).
The next entry, in 1796, is also sited in White Hart Street in which a Robert Dodman, wheelwright, certifies that a certain building, formerly used as a hay barn and called a hay house and now *in part newly erected and enlarged* standing in the yard belonging to his now dwelling house......is by him designed and set apart as a place of religious worship for protestant dissenters. We know no more about its history.
In the nineteenth century other meeting houses were licensed for congregations of Protestants:
1830 - Meeting house in Unicorn Yard. (Primitive Methodist)
1841 - Dwelling and premises in Millgate in occupation of John Skidmore
1842 - New Wesleyan Chapel in White Hart Street.
1844 - House and premises in Millgate in occupation of Benjamin Southgate.
1850 - Cottage and premises in Commercial Road (now Bure Way) in occupation of John Thaxter.
1851 - A room in Red Lion Street occupied by William Smith. (Mission room for Plymouth Brethren).
We do not know how long these remained places of worship.

A Short Review of the history of the present churches and their buildings.

1. The Parish Church of St. Michael and All Angels by the Market Place.
2. Emmanuel Church, White Hart Street, formerly the Baptist Church (and now incorporating
Cawston Road Chapel - see separate entry)
This is Richard Jex's purpose built meeting house. The siting of the building, set back from the street and half hidden by other buildings, is typical of many early chapels. Such secluded locations were chosen at least partly from a desire to keep a low profile and avoid hostility.

The Baptist belief is that this property was built by a Mr. Wilkes, a speculative builder. Certainly Baptists were active in Aylsham at this time. The prime mover was Rev. Joseph Kinghorn of St. Mary's in Norwich; Baptist records show that members from there were coming to Aylsham in 1787. In 1791 he baptised five "believers" in the River Bure on 22nd April at 4am "circumstances rendering it necessary that there should be no bustle about it". Certainly, too, Mr. Kinghorn seems to have been using the building for teaching purposes as well as for Sunday worship.

In 1791 Richard Jex sold the meeting house building to John Boardman, a merchant in Gorleston, (we do not know his denomination) and he in turn sold it to Mrs Mary Berry in 1796.

Both Methodist and Baptist histories tell of an event in 1807 or 1808 in which the chapel was broken into by a riotous crowd during worship and the preacher carried off and held captive in a local hostelry. The Methodists identify him as a visiting minister from Walsingham and the inn as the Dog. At this time the property belonged to Mary Berry.

By 1811 the property had passed from Mary Berry to Mr. Kinghorn and by 1826 to the Trustees of the Baptist Church. The first minister was John Bane, friend of Joseph Kinghorn. He lived in Hungate (now No. 46) and married into the Harvey family - founders and pillars of the church for three generations.

The "New Church" 1796 - 1811

As stated above, Mrs. Mary Berry bought the property in 1796 from John Boardman. She was a lifelong friend of the well known Clover family, who were grocers on the corner of the market place and Hungate. From her correspondence we know she wished the meeting house to become one of the Churches of the New Jerusalem set up by the followers of Emmanuel Swedenborg from about 1750.

Trustees for the New Church were appointed - her daughter, Ann, engaged to marry the artist Joseph Clover, his uncle Thomas Clover, grocer in the Market Place and Dr. Saunders of Norfolk House. Mrs. Berry, a property holder of some substance, had firm ideas about the financing of the church and about the education of the children of poor parents attending the New Church. She mentions a Mr. Crowther as a possible teacher for them.

We do not know whether, or for how long people met for worship there in the new tradition. We know that her daughter died in 1801 and Mr. Thomas Clover in 1803 so maybe she just gave up the project.

John Wright Clover who inherited the grocery business continued as a supporter of the Swedenborgian church as did his artist brother Joseph in London.

Independents (Congregationalists)

Another figure representing Dissent from 1790 onwards was Mr. Samuel Crowther, an Independent minister known to be preaching in Aylsham around 1791. He became minister of Oulton Congregational Chapel. Interestingly, he married, in swift succession, two sisters whose name was Boardman. Was this the same Mr. Crowther mentioned by Mrs. Berry as a possible teacher for the New Church children?

3. Methodist Church, White Hart Street.

Little is known of the history of Methodism in Aylsham between the building of Richard Jex's meeting house in 1789 and the erection of the present building in 1842, the outcome of the enterprise and determination of William Hall. He bought the land, and leased the building to twelve trustees, having mortgaged his own property to finance the operation. The trustees finally purchased the property in 1858. The present facade and other renovations date from 1910.

4. The Roman Catholic Church of St. John of the Cross, White Hart Street.

This was built c. 1900 in the grounds of Abbot's House, White Hart Street by members of the Shepheard family of Abbot's Hall. It has since been enlarged.

5. The Aylsham Tabernacle Church, Millgate.

This was built in 1868 and was one of the thirteen churches which made up the Cawston Circuit attached to the Wesleyan Reform Union. Later this Union broke away from the original Wesleyan (now Methodist) denomination. By 1988 the church had broken its links with the W.R. Union and the Circuit completely. A growing membership led to the buying of a site for a new building in 1991 and in 1992 the new 'resource centre' built in Norwich Road was opened and named:-

6. The Aylsham Tab Community Church

7. The Salvation Army, Mill Road.

The Aylsham Corps opened on 5th July 1886 in premises adjoining Collegiate House on Hungate, its Hall being the former schoolroom of Collegiate House School.

8. Primitive Methodist Chapel, Mill Road.

This chapel was established In 1830 and rebuilt, probably on the same site, in 1887. It was closed in 1932 at the time of the Methodist Union. During the second world war the building was used as a British Restaurant and was sold in 1960 by the Methodists to the Freemasons.

9. Cawston Road Chapel.

This chapel was built in 1891 for George Pretty Esq. for the Plymouth Brethren. The architects were George Skipper FRIBA and F.W. Skipper of Norwich. More recently described as a Gospel Hall or Free Church, its members united with Emmanuel Church in 1994.

10. Religious Society of Friends (Quakers).

Friends Meeting House, Pegg's Yard, Red Lion Street. Friends have been meeting in the town in hired premises since 1984. The Meeting House was purchased and opened as a place of worship in 1994.

References:
St. Michael's Church: *Look at St. Michael's.*
Ede, Virgoe and Williamson: *Halls of Zion*, Centre of East Anglian Studies, 1994
Aylsham Baptist Church: *Bicentenary 1791-1991 publication.*
Methodist Church, Aylsham: *A short history of the buildings, 1784-1884.*
'History of the 'Tab' 1868-1990.
Clover family: Papers of Joseph Clover of Colby NRO MC 2, MC 115, MC 119
        Letters of Mrs. Mary Berry MS 10721 28F
        Bond of Sale of Meeting House - 1796 from John Boardman to
        Mrs. Mary Berry MC 119/20   596x1.

The Norwich to Cromer Turnpike Road

The first section, from Norwich to Aylsham, was begun in 1794. In 1811 the road was extended from Aylsham to Cromer.
Toll houses and gates were built:-

"at or near the Two Mile Stone from Norwich"

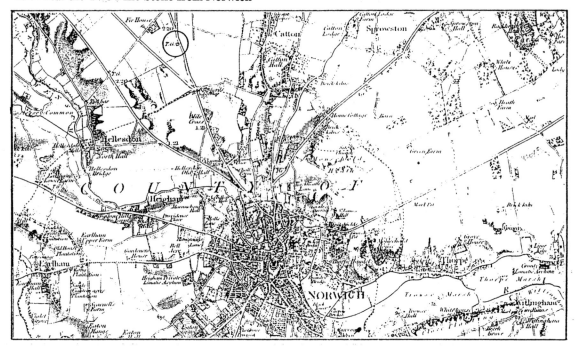

"at or near Ingworth Bridge".　　　　　　　　"on the east side of the road at or near Mill Hill Piece".

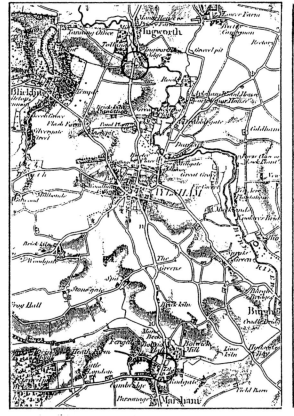
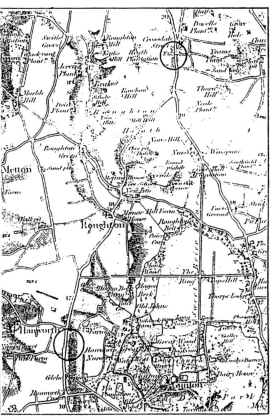

"at or near the Brook upon Marsham Common".　　　at Hanworth in 1811, but discontinued in 1831.

A Scale of tolls was drawn up in 1794 and amended in 1811.

Turnpike Tolls

	1794	1811
For every horse, mare, gelding, mule or ass laden or unladen and not drawing	½d	1d

For every coach, berlin, landau, chariot, caravan, hearse, litter, calash, chaise or other such like carriage (1811 added sociable, barouche, phaeton, curricle, gig, taxed cart and every carriage on springs) drawn by:-

	1794	1811
Six or more horses	4d	1s 3d
Four or three horses		1s 0d
Two horses	3d	6d

For every waggon, wain, dray, cart or such like carriage having the fellies of the wheels of less breadth or gauge than nine inches from side to side, drawn by;-

	1794	1811
Four horses	6d	8d
Three horses	4d	6d
Two horses	3d	4d
One horse	1½d	3d

For every such waggon last mentioned having the fellies of nine inches and upwards drawn by:-

	1794	1811
Eight or seven horses	6d	6d
Six or five horses	4½d	4d
Four, three or two horses	3d	3d

For every waggon or wain last mentioned having fellies of less than six inches laden with millstones or stone or timber drawn by:-

	1811
Four or three horses	1s 0d

For every drove of calves, hogs, sheep or lambs per score and so in proportion for any less number:-

1794	1811
2½d	4d

Exemptions from Turnpike Tolls

Agricultural purposes	Attending divine service
Attending funerals	Conveyance of mails
Military use	Voting at elections
Yeomanry or Volunteers in uniform on exercise	Parson visiting parishioners

A new category of vehicle was added to those liable to pay tolls in 1834:-

Additional Tolls - 1834

For every four wheeled carriage not drawn by any horse or beast of draught but propelled by machinery	1s 6d
For every two wheeled carriage not drawn by any horse or beast of draught but propelled by machinery	9d

The Norwich to Cromer Turnpike Trust ceased to exist in 1876 and the balance of money in hand after payment of expenses was distributed in 1877 among the parishes through which the turnpike road had passed.

The Norwich to Cromer Tramway

When the railways eventually arrived in Aylsham, we ended up with two lines, two stations and two choices of route to get us into Norwich. Despite the choice of two routes, neither of them was particularly direct, and both involved a circuitous journey into the city.

I suspect that it is not widely known, but we could quite easily have avoided all these complications if only the plans of the East Norfolk Tramways Company Ltd. had come to fruition. We could then have enjoyed a tram ride directly to the city by the shortest and most direct route i.e. from Aylsham Market Place, along the main Norwich road (A140) up to St. Augustine's Gate. If we had fancied a trip to Cromer, we could have caught a tram in the opposite direction right into Cromer town centre. All this would have been possible some ten years before the railways arrived in town.

What little we know today of the proposed tramway is contained in the records now preserved in the Town archives. There, we have two books of plans of all the proposed sections of the tramway showing the whole of the route from Norwich to Cromer. It was to have started in Norwich in the parish of St.Clement Without, "opposite the entrance gate to the Green Hills Public House" which was near to the present day Aylsham Rd/Drayton Road junction. It would have followed the present Aylsham Road out of the city, crossing what is now Norwich Airport by the old Norwich road to St.Faiths, then through Hainford, Hevingham, Marsham, Aylsham, Ingworth, Erpingham, Roughton to its terminus in Cromer, at a point in a field known as Baker's Field belonging to B.Bond Cabbell Esq.

The tramway was designed for the purpose of conveying passengers, animals, goods, minerals and parcels. We can visualise how passengers might have been conveyed, but one wonders what sort of rolling stock would have been used to convey the rest. The proposals also specified a single track serving the route, except for turn outs or passing places. It was certainly envisaged as a true tramway (not a light railway) sharing the same road way as all other forms of transport. The provisions of the Order are quite clear, and stipulate that "The uppermost surface of the rail to be level with the road surface"

There were five sidings or passing places planned along the route, as follows:-
1.   At St. Faiths at a point near the junction of the Horsford Road with the Norwich to Aylsham Turnpike.
2.   At Hainford at the milestone, 6 miles from Norwich.
3.   At Marsham, at or near the junction of the Cawston Road with the Aylsham - Norwich Turnpike.
4.   At Erpingham, at or near the milestone, Norwich 14 miles/Cromer 6m.
5.   At Roughton, 5 chains south of the New Inn.

Arrangements for the route through Aylsham seem quite bizarre. The tramway would have entered along the Norwich Road, but at the Dog corner (Burgh Rd. junction) it was to have turned right into Burgh Rd., then left into Oakfield Rd., down the hill past the gas works, then left into Bure

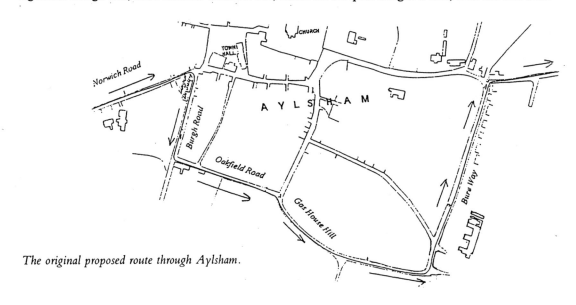

The original proposed route through Aylsham.

Way. At the end of Bure Way it would have re-joined the Turnpike for the rest of its journey. The building which stands at the corner of Norwich Rd/Burgh Rd. was earmarked as a site for sheds and stables etc. for the Company's vehicles. A compulsory purchase order was included in the proposals for that purpose.

Yes, stables! I hadn't mentioned that it would have been a horse-drawn tramway, of course, and how long the journey would have taken is hard to imagine. The only printed description of the proposed tramway is contained in the Draft Provisional Order which was prepared for approval by Parliament in 1873. In the draft there is nothing to suggest what form of propulsion was proposed, but the provision of stabling etc., suggests that horse trams were intended. It was far too early for electricity to have been considered, in fact the first electric tramway in England was still 20 years away in the future, when the city of Leeds installed its electric tramway in 1891.

The whole route would have followed the turnpike, and the existing plans which show the whole route are useful in that they also illustrate the features of the turnpike. A considerable amount of work must have gone into the preparation of the plans, which are very detailed. They spell out quite clearly how far the track should be from the centre line of the roadway, and the angles of curves and gradients. Arrangements are made for the compulsory purchase of land and buildings, if necessary.

All of these meticulous plans were drawn by the engineer, Mr. Leslie Jeyes. Copies of plans of the relevant sections were sent to the Parish Clerk of each parish through which the route passed, and a complete set of all documents and plans were deposited "on the 30th. day of November, 1871 with the Clerk of the Peace for the said county". A note confirming that this had been done is signed by Charles Foster on the cover of the Aylsham copy of the plans.

What happened next? The short answer is we simply do not know! Two things did happen that we know of; one was that the proposers of the tramway were also submitting plans for another tramway system which would have run from Norwich to Taverham. The starting point for both routes would have been the same, i.e. opposite the Green Hills Public House, outside St. Augustine's Gate. The two routes would have split almost immediately, with the route for Taverham heading off down the Drayton Road.

I have not come across any plans or drawings for this second route, although they must have been prepared, in a similar form to those for the Cromer route. The Eastern Daily Press for 22nd. January 1872 confirms that the Norwich - Costessey - Taverham scheme had been approved by the Board of Trade. A Local Act was also approved by Parliament sanctioning the same scheme. I have not found any record of the Cromer scheme receiving Parliamentary approval, but the Cromer scheme arrangements had certainly not gone dead. The second event to take place at this time was a fresh look at the proposed route of the Cromer tramway. The second set of plans in the Aylsham Archives are dated one year later and reveal completely fresh proposals for the route through Aylsham. The original peculiar routing had been abandoned and a much more direct and logical route substituted.

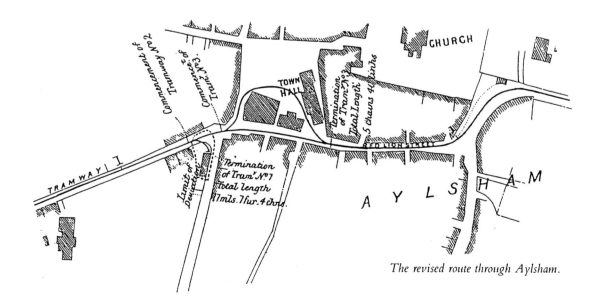

The revised route through Aylsham.

Now, the route was to split at the Dog corner with one line continuing along Red Lion Street, and another line turning left into the Market Place with a stopping and passing place positioned just about where the bus stop is today. This second line would have completed its route through the Market Place to join up with the other line in Red Lion Street. This certainly seems a more logical proposal, although on the return journey, the old horse would have had its work cut out climbing up the hill into town!

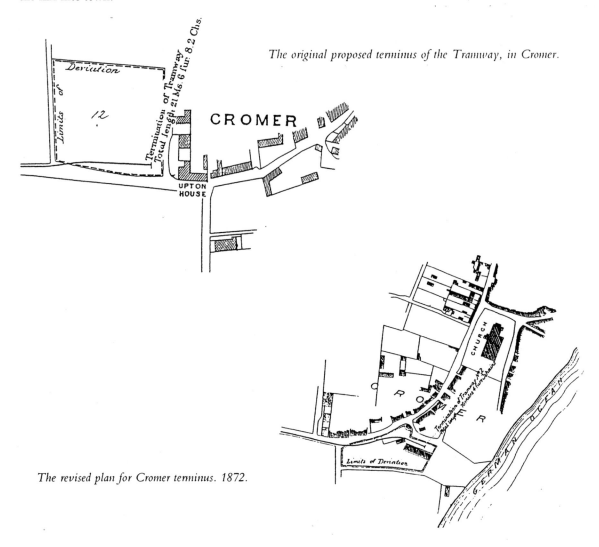

The original proposed terminus of the Tramway, in Cromer.

The revised plan for Cromer terminus. 1872.

The plans for the terminus at Cromer were also considerably revised. The 1871 plan shows the route ending near Upton House, roughly where the Overstrand Road joins the Norwich Road near the traffic lights. The 1872 plan, however, takes the line a little further into town towards Church Street, turning into the Gangway, and ending behind the present East Coast Motors Garage. Incidentally, the line of the tramway along the Norwich Road had been shifted from one side of the road to the other. It is also interesting to read on the plans that passengers dismounting at the Cromer terminus would have been just a few short steps from the German Ocean'. This was 1872; when did we begin to call it the North Sea'?

Despite the revisions of the proposed route nothing ever happened with either proposed tramway. There seems to be no record of what eventually killed the idea off. Possibly the proposers were already hearing rumours of the Great Eastern's plans to bring the railway into Aylsham, and wisely dropped their own proposals. What a pity - it would have made a wonderful day out from Norwich unless, of course, you happened to be a horse.

Railway Memorabilia

This collection of memorabilia has been presented by us several times over the past few years, namely at Gressenhall, Blickling, Aylsham Town Hall and Bure Valley Railway Station at their Steam Gala Weekends. It consists of photographs going back to the last century, the oldest shows Aylsham as a terminus in 1880, before the railway was extended beyond Cawston. Other photographs cover the first world war and between the wars, as well as pictures taken by us from 1986 to 1990, before the destruction of the Victorian station buildings, together with maps drawn by the late Ivan Morris, a prominent member of the Aylsham Local History Society. In the collection there is an engine man's uniform, boilerwasher's clogs, oil feeders, a detonator case, examiner's gas lamp, a fireman's coal hammer and shovel, a leather Great Eastern wages bag, two union badges, one for the National Union of Railwaymen and the other for ASLEF, The Associated Society of Locomotive Engineers and Firemen, but always referred to by its members as "The Associated".

Oil Lamps

An important part of the railway memorabilia is the oil lamp, the railway management in the past was firmly wedded to the oil lamp, there was nothing like it. Foreign railways had electric lamps on their engines, but the fastest steam locomotive in the world was still equipped with oil lamps, even diesel electric pilots were fitted with oil lamps and we had a vast selection - semaphore signals, ground signals, known as Dods, short for Tommy Dod, gate, head, tail and gaugelamps. There were also lamps in huts, signal boxes, waiting rooms, platforms, station drives and the very important hand lamps which were used by shunters and guards. These last ones had red and green shades. Shunters at night had to use a shunting pole which required the use of both hands, they also had to work a hand lamp to instruct the driver, consequently their casualty rate was second to coal miners when railways were at the height of their activity.

Engine men and fitters used torches, known in some quarters as flare lamps, the torches were used for preparing and disposing of engines. When you had an oil feeder in one hand and a torch in the other, the combination was alright outside but not so good inside, then you had to be careful not to set yourself on fire! We even used these lamps in the blackout. In the last days of the old railway companies 1945 - 1946 new engines came out with electric lighting sets. The first ones used a 6 volt system with batteries and a hub dynamo, they were fitted to one of the front bogie wheels rather like a bicycle, but they were not a success. After this, engines were fitted with a 24 volt system, powered with a Stones Turbo Generator and were without batteries. While the system was properly maintained they were successful! When the railways were nationalized the new BR engines went back to oil lamps. The trouble with the oil lamps on Britannia Pacific's occurred when they were in the head code for the express passenger position. When the engine passed another train on the opposite line, the updraft from the smoke deflector put the lamps out. Before World War 2 the Cambridge had a very modern electric signalling system with power operated points and signals, but they still had semaphore boards with oil lamps.

Examiners Gas Lamp

Known to the public as wheeltappers examiners they are not at all like Will Hay in 'Oh Mr. Porter' and were in fact responsible men in charge of the fitting staff. Those seen by passengers were the carriage and waggon examiners, there were also locomotive examiners whom the passengers did not see and they used electric and not carbide lamps.

Engine Men's Uniform

This consisted of a cap, set of overalls, a serge jacket and the last 'steam men's' uniform issued by British Rail. In Great Eastern days the only clothing issued by the company were greatcoats. The usual driver's wear was a bowler hat, dark jacket and cord trousers which were washed weekly until they were almost white; they also carried an umbrella and a brief case. There was a woman in Norwich who undertook the washing of drivers cords and it was said that by the end of the week you could just see where he had rested his hands on his knees, - engines were clean in those days. A lot of fireman wore old police uniforms which were bought from a shop near Liverpool Street station.

Clogs

A thing which seems to interest many people is a pair of boiler washer's clogs. Clogs were also worn by brewery workers and other people working in cold wet conditions and they were more comfortable than they looked, once one became used to them.

Detonator Cases

The detonator case contains 12 detonators and 2 red flags and these were carried on engines for emergency use in case of obstruction, break down or derailment etc. The fireman went forward and the guard went back, and he had his own detonators and flags. One detonator was laid at ¾ of a mile, one at ½ a mile and three at ¼ of a mile to warn assisting engines or oncoming traffic if the opposite line was also obstructed, that is if there was time.

Detonators were painted in different colours to denote the year of issue and the colour changed every three years. It was at one time part of my job to inspect them for any over-aged or damaged detonators. The detonators called 'fogs' by station staff and platelayers, were domed-shaped objects, the width of the rail with a lead strip to hold it in place; they contained about 3 drams of medium black powder, and a metal ring with 5 dummy nipples fitted with percussion caps and they were very reliable. They were formerly used to give the position of signals in bad visibility, i.e. fog or falling snow. Since the advent of automatic systems they are now only used in an emergency.

Engine Tools

Several tools are carried on steam engines, the most important being the fireman's shovel. These came in different lengths, the shortest for tank engines and the longest for the "Belpaire Boiler 1500's". This was said to have a tuppenny bus ride for the shovel, between the plate on the tender and the tube plate at the front of the firebox. It was not unknown for the fireman to let the shovel go into the firebox and by the time he had recovered it, it was not much use, so if there were not some old shovels on the back of the tender, you had to borrow one from the platelayers, but platelayers shovels were a different form. The coal hammer was very awkward to use, it had a square on one side and a pick on the other, rather like a martel. We also had a bucket for carrying tools in or washing etc. and a hand brush for sweeping up the footboard. Two oil feeders and four oil bottles, one for engine oil, one for black oil (cylinder oil), one for paraffin for head lights and one for heavy petroleum for the gauge lamp. If paraffin was put in the gauge lamp it became too hot and the vessel would ignite. There were two kinds of black oil, ordinary cylinder oil for wet steam (unsuper heated) engines, the J15 etc. which was a dark green colour, and the super heated cylinder oil which was a dark brown and for dry steam engines. The super heat oil was more commonly used than the ordinary oil.

Oil feeders had no way of stopping the flow of oil except by bringing them back to the horizontal. To do this there were various spanners. Spanners included an adjustable known as a pair of monkeys and a ¾" Whitworth; there was also a Donkey Spanner, for the Westinghouse Air Compressor, where they were fitted. If you were lucky, you had a donkey, but if not you had to use the monkeys, which was detrimental to the Donkey Lubricator Cap, which was made of brass and after a while became rounded. We also had a supply of boiler gauge glasses and spare corks for the various lubrication points and a container of detonators and of course the headlamps. These had to be drawn from the stores, carried down to the engine, which could be a few hundred yards away, and then returned to the store. There was also a set of fire irons and a shute for the firebox door which were left on the engine. The set of fire irons were a slice, a pricker and a bent dart. The slice, is a kind of shovel on a long iron shaft and it was used for turning the fire over or for throwing it out. The pricker was for breaking up the clinker that formed on the bars or for getting the fire out of the back corners, and the dart which was about twelve feet long and had a U shaped head at a right angle to the handle, was used to dislodge the fire from the back corners of the fire box and from the corners under the back of the fire box door. I remember the darts that were used on the Great Northern Atlantics, they were the only engines I knew that used straight darts; they were also made of cast iron and consequently very heavy to use.

The Aylsham Regatta and Rowing Club

The scene on the Society's post card and the cover of this book shows the Aylsham Regatta painted by Walter Mileham in 1850.

The point where Mileham painted the regatta is uncertain. Contemporary reports place it above the road bridge at Millgate, on the stretch of river close to where the railway bridge crosses the river. In the intervening years the area has radically changed and the railway bridge is now part of the Weavers Way. Some of the trees that grew in Mileham's time have disappeared and today there are many more trees along that stretch of the river bank.

This first regatta was won by Dr R K Morton's "Fairy Queen" and at a meeting held at the Anchor Inn on the 9th of May 1851 the Aylsham Aquatic Club was launched. Its object was to "promote sailing and rowing matches between members". The first president was Mr Samuel Parmeter and the Commodore, Dr Fred Smith. The club also had its own flag, an eight pointed white star on a red ground.

There were a number of regattas arranged by the club, but these all seem to have been held on the Aylsham Navigation Company's canal between the basin and the lock. The 1850 regatta may have been the only one held on the River Bure.

On the 9th of June 1871 the Aylsham Aquatic Club was reformed and the name was changed to "The Aylsham and Buxton Rowing Club". The club's new Commodore was Dr R.K. Morton, and monthly meetings were held in The Red Lion Hotel. During the summer months regattas continued to be held at Aylsham, but on the 11th of September 1872 a more ambitious regatta was held further down river at Buxton. At this meeting a sailing and three rowing matches were held, and curiously the meeting finished with a steeplechase, which crossed the river at some point, but the exact location is unknown.

The club was wound up in 1876 after trouble with six young men who were members of the club and were a persistent source of trouble and embarrassment to the other members. They damaged the club boat, broke oars, lost rowlocks and left "the boat in such a filthy condition, not fit for a lady to sit in."

Walter Mileham the amateur painter was also an amateur poet and included here is his not too serious tribute to the Aylsham Festivities, which were held to celebrate Queen Victoria's Coronation.

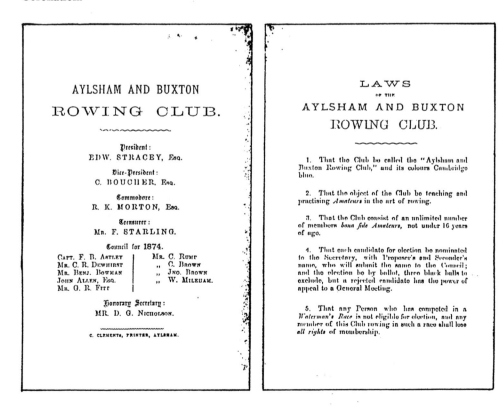

THE

AYLSHAM CORONATION FESTIVAL,

June 28th, 29th, and 30th, 1838.

The Frenchman may boast of his three glorious days,
　And toast them in bumpers of wine ;
But as feasting beats fighting, I'll fill up my glass,
　Be " The Aylsham Festivities" mine.
In honour of Britain's fair Queen of the Isles,
　Every heart glowed with pure exultation.
And the pale yellow morning was greeted with smiles,
　That witnessed our Queen's coronation.

Our merry bells trolled forth a right loyal peal,
　From their tower decked with branches so green ;
Whilst the streamers and flags as they danced in the breeze,
　Seemed to welcome Victoria our Queen.
It appeared as if some great magician of old,
　Had arisen to favour our station ;
And had touched with his wand every house, street and place,
　To honour our Queen's coronation.

For the fair band of Flora, the market had dressed,
　Verdant arches triumphal were made ;
A perfect Arcadia the town looked to be,
　And the streets like some old forest glade.
Boughs, pictures, buds, stars, garlands, crowns, and V. R's.
　Were displayed with a proud emulation ;
At the call of the bugle, the cry was away
　To the feast of our Queen's coronation.

Sixteen hundred with beef, good plum puddings and ale
　Were provided—how joyous the scene !
And the knives and the forks, what sweet music they made,
　As the band struck up, " God save the Queen."
Then the health of Victoria was drank with six cheers !
　And three more ! !—with renewed approbation.
Oh ! many glad hearts who that day drank the toast,
　Will remember the Queen's coronation.

Porter, pipes and tobacco next crowned the gay board,
　(We all know what comfort these yield,)
And as evening drew on, Pleasure's votaries retired.
　To enjoy rustic sports in a field.
Here the light country dance, climbing up the soaped pole,
　Kept the concourse in high excitation ;
With the jingling match, races, and jumping in sacks,
　Closed the day of the Queen's coronation.

Her majesty next day was chaired in full state,
　Victoria, of rare Aylsham town ;
And if for the task she a sovereign received,
　The Queen beat—as she got but a *crown.*
When the line of procession had finished its march,
　She alighted from her elevation,
Joined the dance till bright sol had long sunk in the west,
　Then guns fired for the Queen's coronation.

The third and last day of this excellent treat,
　Was concluded just as it should be ;
For if with the ladies you wish to keep friends,
　Why give them a cup of good tea ;
Their banner was hoisted—a tea kettle large—
　On a pole, round which all took their station ;
Five hundred " drunk deep" of the best black and green,
　And ALL TALKED of the grand coronation.

The lasses and lads once more tripped on the plain,
　Till the curtains of night closed the scene ;
Then the party broke up, giving three hearty cheers
　For our youthful and kind hearted Queen.
Long, long may she reign in each true Briton's heart,
　Is my loyal and firm exclamation ;
And long may we live to remember the day,
　Of Victoria the Queen's coronation.

W. M.

PRINTED FOR C. CL▢▢▢ ▢LER, &C. AYLSHAM.

Queen Victoria's Diamond Jubilee Celebrations

How the Planning Started

It was at a public meeting held in the Town Hall on 8th June, 1897, that various ways of commemorating the Diamond Jubilee were discussed, despite the fact that the Aylsham Parish Council had only come into existence in December 1894, with the Rev. J. G. Hoare as Chairman.

Mr R. J. W. Purdy was strongly in favour of a recreation ground for the parish as a permanent memorial and he was supported by Mr. B. Cook. Mr. Cook, however, also considered the youngsters of the town should have a tea on the evening of Jubilee Day. The Vicar also wished to give a tea to all the aged and infirm people. After discussion of these proposals, it was agreed that there should be tea and sports for children under 14 years of age and that the old people should be invited to join in. A Committee was then formed to carry out the details and a subscription list opened.

Twelve days later a large procession marched round the town before a Church Service.
Fourteen days later Aylsham celebrated with a

    Dinner for 1800 people

    Sports

    Bonfire

    Fireworks

    Dancing

as reported in the Eastern Daily Press of June 23rd, 1897, and later described very fully in the Aylsham Almanac of 1898 by Mr. Harry F. Proudfoot, Secretary of the Jubilee Committee. People were informed by a poster, the Town Crier and by a visit from a Committee Member.

Finances

At the public meeting a Subscription List was opened and amounts varying from 6d to £10 were promised. Over the next two weeks about 120 people paid £93.1s.4d. Special 6d tickets were printed and 767 people bought these tickets amounting to £19.3s.6d. An amount of £9.11s.9d. had been left over from the Jubilee Dinner of 1887 and this was added. Since a deficit of £9.1s.4d. still remained, eight members of the Festival Committee paid further subscriptions.

The Secretary, Mr. H. Proudfoot, kept careful details of all bills and these shed further light on the preparations and clearing up of the Dinner and Sports. The total expenditure was £130.17s.11d. It would appear that 750 children and old people received free meals so possibly the figure mentioned in the EDP report of 1,600 inhabitants sitting down to dinner is accurate. The population of Aylsham at this time was approximately 2,500.

The year 1897 is now considered by historians to be the lowest point of the agricultural depression affecting Great Britain in the late 19th and early 20th centuries. It seems that 900 people either could not afford the 6d. dinner ticket or did not wish to join that part of the Diamond Jubilee Celebrations. There were, of course, special celebrations taking place in Norwich and other nearby towns.

Committee members each visited a section of the town to obtain the accurate numbers of old people and children under 14.
Free tickets issued to men and Women over 60 years of age and children under 14

Area visited	By whom	Over 60	Under 14
All that part of Millgate beyond Water Bridge and from Water Bridge to Gas House and Town Lane including Muckland	Mr Cook and Mr Aldous	36	154
Commercial Rd., Doctor's Meadows, Cromer Rd. to Mr Denmark's, Peterson's Lane & Blickling Rd. to Police Station & School Lane	Mr Starling	13	28
From Gas House to Miss Larners, Town Lane & White Hart St terminating at Mr Miller's shoemakers & Mrs Goulders on the Hill	Mr E J Bird	32	60
Red Lion St to Rev Ford's, including from Mrs Peel, Church Hill	Mr W F White	4	30

Burgh Rd., Norwich Rd. from Rev Ford's, Spratts Green and to Bolwick Hall Cottages	Mr J Partridge	7	32
Market Place incl. Dyes Loke, Church Terr. & Penfold St	Mr R H Ward	5	10
Hungate St from Mr Bond's round by Le Neves, incl. Unicorn Yard, Carr's Corner & Buttlands	Mr H Page	27	75
The Rookery, Hungate St, by Yaxleys Lane round by Smithson's house & Mill Rd. to Swan Corner	Mr S Bruce	22	31
Cawston Rd. from Engine House to Bridge inc. Fox Loke	Mr A S White	25	35
Pound Roads	Mr J Goulder	9	26
From Cawston Rd. Bridge to Spa. Heydon Rd. & outlying districts	Mr B B Sapwell	6	20
		186	**501**

Food

Although it was resolved to ask for tenders for the children's tea (tea, bread and butter, sandwiches, beef patties and cake) and the old people's tea (tea, bread and butter, joints of cold meat, pickles, hot plum puddings and cake), the Food Sub-Committee decided to buy supplies from at least four butchers and as many bakers. Mr Page put his house at the disposal of the Committee for making plum puddings. Eight ladies, the wives of committee members, were appointed to cook 128 puddings, each weighing 6 lbs. Three women were paid to help them. Mr Cross and Mr Goulder bought the meat. Mr Proudfoot noted that there was a plentiful supply of all kinds of meat with roast beef at every table and salt beef and roast mutton at every other table. Mr Ducker was asked to provide 5 barrels of Worthington J beer at 30/- a barrel. Mr Wright was deputed to see that the tables were put up and covered with cloths and to see that the Market Place was "watered".

Sports

The Sports Committee was responsible for the bonfire, the sports and the salute of guns. Prizes for races included 5/-for the first in Men's Over 50 race and 10/- for the Tug of War winners.

Queen Victoria's Diamond Jubilee Celebrations

The following report in the AYLSHAM ALMANAC OF 1898 by Mr Harry F Proudfoot, Secretary of the Jubilee Committee, gives an excellent review of the Celebrations.

CELEBRATION OF THE QUEEN'S DIAMOND JUBILEE

AT AYLSHAM, 1897.

ON Tuesday, June 8th, 1897, at 7.30 p.m., a large and enthusiastic Meeting was held in the Town Hall to consider what steps should be taken to celebrate the Queen's Diamond Jubilee.

Mr. William Forster was unanimously voted to the chair, and in opening the proceedings he said he would, unfortunately, be away at the time of the celebration, but he would co-operate in whatever the Meeting resolved to do.

A committee was then formed to carry out details, consisting of Messrs. H. G. Wright, B. Cook, H. J. Gidney, S. B. Sapwell, J. Goulder, (Revs. J. G. Hoare and J. H. Cole), I. Page, F. W. Starling, S. E. Bruce, E. D. Browne, I. Marjoram, W. F. White, D. G. Nicholson, A. R. Cuddenham, R. H. Ward, E. J. Bird, S. D. Bone, V. Jackson, and J. Partridge, with Mr. Harry F. Proudfoot as Secretary.

At a committee meeting held on the Monday following it was unanimously resolved that a Dinner take place in the Market Place at 4 o'clock on Tuesday, June 22nd, and that children under 15 and aged people over 60 years of age be admitted free; persons between those ages to be admitted on payment of Sixpence.

There was a balance in hand from 1887 Jubilee Fund of £9 11s. 9d., and Mr. Wm. Forster offered the sum of £10 as a start to the new subscription list.

BALANCE SHEET.

RECEIVED.	£	s.	d.	PAID.	£	s.	d.
By Subscriptions	102	2	8	Bills according to statement	.. 130	17	11
,, 767 tickets sold at 6d. each	19	3	6				
Balance of 1887 Jubilee Fund	9	11	9				
	£130	17	11		£130	17	11

QUANTITIES OF EATABLES SUPPLIED.

637 lbs. Roast Beef ⎫
310 lbs. Salt Beef ⎬ 1,301 lbs.
354 lbs. Mutton ⎪
187 lbs. Suet ⎭

The amount of £51 7s. 1d. was paid for the above.

39 stone of Bread, 178½ pts. Milk, 84 lbs. Salt, 12 gallons Pickles, 184 lbs. Sugar, 187 lbs. Raisins, 100 lbs. Currants, 33 lbs. Candid Peel, 326 lbs. Flour, 180 gallons Beer. Tea and Lemonade was also supplied.

There were 60 tables erected in the Market Place, with accommodation for 30 people at each.

The Aylsham Band being engaged, the Cawston Band of 8 performers was hired at the sum of £3.

The Ringers gave several merry peals upon the Church Bells during the day.

There were made for the Dinner 190 6-lb. Plum Puddings—a plenty for all and to spare.

On June 22nd, 1897, about 1800 people sat down to dinner in the Market Place at 4 p.m., the weather being all that one could desire, in fact, quite Queen's weather.

Several of the inhabitants had decorated their premises, and the Market Place looked beautiful with its adornment of flags and bunting, and what with the tables covered with their floral garb, the sight was one that the youngest inhabitant will not soon forget.

After dinner, Rustic Sports, &c., were held on a meadow kindly lent for the occasion by Mr. George Durrell, and at 10 o'clock a great Bonfire was lighted, Fireworks were

displayed, and the Church Tower was beautifully illuminated. The Market Place was also illuminated with Stars, Shields, Chinese Lanterns, &c. Dancing was indulged in until a late hour.

It is pleasing to record that everything passed off without the slightest hitch or accident of any kind, and although until a fortnight before the 22nd of June no steps had been taken to celebrate the Jubilee, in the space of that fortnight work was done quickly and well, the committee combining together with the ladies' committee, consisting of Mesdames Cook, Little, Gidney, Ward, Starling, Sapwell, and Hoare, who, in no small way, helped toward the successful issue of the celebration.

It must also be put on record that the celebration commenced on Sunday, June 20th. At 5 o'clock, p.m., a procession was formed in the Vicarage grounds, consisting of the 3rd V.B.N.R., headed by the Band, Major Gidney in command; the Parish Council; Fire Brigade and Engine; the various Benefit Societies with regalia; the School Children carrying flags.

This procession, after parading the principal streets of the town, assembled for Divine Service in the old Parish Church, when a sermon for the occasion was preached by the Vicar, the Rev. J. Gurney Hoare.

HARRY F. PROUDFOOT,
Secretary of Jubilee Committee.

Photographs taken by Dr Bansall before and during the dinner

Flooding at Mash's Row 1993

In his book, 'The History of Aylsham' John Sapwell writes of one of the worst natural disasters to visit Norfolk which occurred on Monday, 26th August 1912, when following a fortnight of wet weather, 7½ inches of rain fell in twenty four hours, accompanied by a north west gale. He also writes that as a result of this heavy rainfall, Mash's Row was flooded to first floor level and the occupiers had to be rescued by boat.

The events of the flood of 1912 have certain similarities to the flood in Mash's Row on the 13th October 1993 as in both cases, homes were flooded to a depth of between 20 inches to 32 inches and the last residents had to be taken out by boat. The summer months of 1993 had produced a considerable rainfall which had not been totally absorbed into the land and on the 12th and 13th of October, it rained both day and night. This rainwater increased the level of the River Bure and its outlets and additional water drained from the land into the river. On the evening of the 13th October, the River Bure burst its bank in two places in Drabblegate, flooding the gardens of the houses and cottages and then flowed in a torrent across two fields towards Mash's Row. At the old railway line embankment, which is now the Weavers Way, the water flowed through an arch under a bridge, spread out over the land and engulfed the rear of Mash's Row. This torrent of water, flooded the houses and cottages and swept forward to the junction at Dunkirk where it flooded part of the industrial estate and the front gardens of the three nearby houses.

At the same time on that evening, the level of the water in the bypass channel, which extends from the weir at the River Bure to the Aylsham Mill, had risen so high that it spread towards the cottages and houses in Mash's Row and caused them to be flooded. There were two reasons for the flooding from the bypass channel and one was due to a lack of maintenance, the channel had become overgrown along the bank and therefore narrower in width. The second reason was that the land opposite the cottages and number one Mash's Row, was overgrown with nettles, grasses, brambles and other weeds. This dense growth forced the water back on to the buildings and added to the flooding. In previous years the growth on this land was kept low, as old photographs show, and had the low level of growth been maintained, as in previous years, the water would have passed across it to the River Bure. The buildings in Mash's Row were therefore flooded from the front and the rear.

The residents of Mash's Row were aware of the possibility of their homes being flooded during the afternoon of the 13th October and spent the next few hours moving as many of their household goods as possible to their upstairs rooms. Although the National Rivers Authority had provided sandbags, these could not prevent the flood water from invading the houses. At 7.30 p.m. the flood water had burst through one of the cottages in Mash's Row and in the following few minutes had flooded all the cottages and the houses in the row. All the residents had either evacuated before the flood water engulfed their homes or had left shortly afterwards, but two residents remained and were taken out by boat the next morning.

On the 15th October, the flood water had completely vanished from Mash's Row and the residents returned to their homes to inspect the damage and start the cleaning up operations. The water had left a residue on walls up to the flood level and on all floor surfaces there was a coating of mud. All carpets and other floor coverings had to be removed and discarded and the floors washed down and cleaned out. The houses and cottages were not habitable as they were not only wet, but all the electrical appliances were affected by the water and were no longer in working order. The Mash's Row residents cleaned up their homes by day and retired to spend the night with relatives or friends. De-humidifier machines were installed in every residence to extract water from the floors and walls, electricians and other maintenance engineers came to repair the equipment which had been damaged in the flood and after four days, the majority of Mash's Row residents had returned to their homes. Every house and cottage has required the installation of new kitchen units, the redecorating of rooms and the replacement of carpets and furniture.

The flood of 1912 destroyed a great deal of the river and the canal system and this change has subsequently affected those living in Mash's Row. The wherries no longer come to Aylsham and the canal that they travelled upon has become neglected and overgrown throughout the years. It is not only the non-maintenance of the river that has contributed to the flooding in Mash's Row, but the changes in farming methods in the surrounding area which have to be taken into consideration. In the period from the 1800's to the mid 1900's, the agricultural fields in Norfolk were relatively small and surrounded by hedges and ditches. Many of the ditches have now gone, and those that remain are overgrown and neglected. The fields are wide open spaces where the soil has been compacted by the weight of heavy agricultural machinery, drainage ditches have disappeared and any excess of rain lies on the land. When this rainfall drains from the land, it drains into the nearest river. This drainage of rainwater takes with it the top soil which silts up the river bed, thus creating further potential flooding problems. In recent years there has been a considerable amount of building in Aylsham, and the drainage from these buildings also flows into the River Bure and adds to the problem at times of heavy rainfall.

The residents of Mash's Row had been concerned for the last two years at the possibility of their homes being flooded as they have witnessed the neglect of the River Bure and the by-pass channel near their homes. Their fears were justified on the 13th October 1993 and they formed an action group within the following week with the aim of preventing any further flooding to their homes. They submitted documentary and photographic evidence to Richard Ryder, their Member of Parliament, who took their complaint to Lord Crickhowell, the Chairman of the National Rivers Authority. It is due to the concern of Richard Ryder and Lord Crickhowell for the residents of Mash's Row that work on the River Bure has been implemented. This has consisted of the NRA, dredging and widening the River Bure from the A140 to Aylsham Mill. The opening up of this area of the river bed has allowed the water from the River Bure to flow past Mash's Row without building up to a high level. Since the October flood, the NRA have carried out work on the by-pass channel from the weir at the far end of Mash's Row to the underpass at the bridge near Bridge House. Further work at the bridge is also to be carried out and this gives the residents some confidence for the future.

This confidence could, however, be undermined, if the River Bure is not maintained in future and the complaisant attitudes of the past are allowed to return. The river banks from Aylsham to Ingworth and further beyond are sadly overgrown and the natural river bed is curtailed, thus preventing the free flow of water. The River Bure in the other direction from Aylsham to Burgh, Oxnead and Buxton has also suffered from a lack of river and drainage maintenance and in recent times, these areas have been flooded.

The cottages in Mash's Row were built in 1845 by William Mash and the present two houses in 1848. They are listed as Grade II buildings and are of historical interest to Aylsham and must be saved from any further damage by flooding.

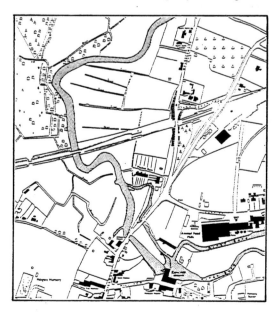

River Bure prior to flooding

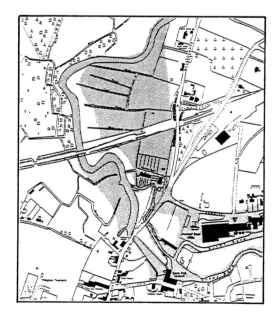

Extent of flooding

Oral History

In April 1993, the Aylsham Local History Society formed an Oral History Group under the chairmanship of Jane Nolan. In the months that have followed, a number of recordings have been made with the older residents of Aylsham. Each recording has been transcribed and the tape and transcript will be added to the collection of the Aylsham Archives and to the Centre of East Anglian Studies Sound Archive. All the material will be preserved as a public reference resource for use in research, and all the contributions are covered by copyright protection.

The Society is grateful to all those who have recorded their memories and given permission for the tapes and transcripts to be used. The following extracts are taken from the recordings of Mrs E. Crouch, Mr R.A. Matthews, Mr C. Spinks, Mr G.H. Baker and Mr A.F. Pull.

Shops

'The biggest store in the town was Henry Page, on the site of the new chemist and fruit shop. I can remember going past two large windows in Hungate and the blinds were drawn when the shop was shut. The blinds were putty coloured, on one was written 'H. Page, Mantles', and on the other, 'H. Page, Millinery'. In the store, cables ran to a central kiosk, which was slightly raised and when you paid your money it was screwed into a container, a miniature bell pull was pulled and the container sped to the kiosk where the girl would return the change in the same container. If the bill came to something three farthings, instead of one farthing change, you were given three miniature brass safety pins. When you made a purchase you were given a silver coloured disk and a collection of disks allowed you to purchase something free.'

'Where Gateways is now, it used to be the International Stores and previously it was the Aylsham Post Office. In the early 30's the manager of the post office was a Mr Bruton, who lived in Hungate. If we passed the scholarship (11+ exam) he would invite us into the post office and give us half a crown as a reward. We thought this was marvellous as a half crown was a fortune. When the new post office was built, there were a lot of alterations to the old post office and the International Stores warehouse which came up to the surgery premises. The International Stores had at one time been in Red Lion Street, it is now an electrical shop'.

Millgate Store

'I left school and was asked by the manager of Dent's store in Millgate if I would like to start there. I started on a Tuesday morning. The money at Dent's was six shillings a week and I went as an apprentice. My first job was weighing up sugar, there were three of us, one would fill the bag, one would weigh and one would wrap. The sugar came in 2cwt. sacks, the moist sugar (brown sugar) came in 1cwt. sacks and the cube sugar in boxes, icing sugar came in 14lb. tins. We would weigh the sugar in 1lb. 2lb. 3lbs. 4lbs. and 6lbs which were sold for two and a half pennies or twopence farthing a pound.

On Mondays, my day would be patting up butter and margarine with two paddles, butter pats. This was done in the cellar where it was cold, there were no fridges in those days and we kept everything down there. We sold eggs, not by the dozen, but by the score and people bought a score or half a score. We had local flour from Barclay and Pallett, Colman's self raising flour, but there was little demand for self raising flour and we mainly sold plain flour. We weighed this up into quarter stones, half stones and one stone. Many people baked their own bread so we often sold a couple of stones of flour at a time. We did deliveries, and a boy had a trade bike and I used to sometimes deliver in the immediate area. We also had an old Ford car which had been converted and had curtains at the sides so you could roll up the curtains and get the groceries. It had a cupboard on the back which had stock, such as jam, mustard, custard powder, baking powder, cocoa, tea and anything people might want. We would go to the villages. We had different rounds, one area for each day of the week. Corpusty and Saxthorpe and villages in between, then Cawston and that area, and Erpingham and Calthorpe. People would order from one week to another, they would put their order in and we would get them ready the day before delivery. If they forgot something, we would have spare goods to help them.'

Children's Games and Empire Day

'When I was a boy, we used to have picnics by the river and in the six weeks holiday from school, you could reckon on between fifty and sixty kiddies would be down by the bridge at Millgate. On the weir there'd be paddling and having a little old handkerchief to go underneath the weeds and get the little fish. On the green, we used to organize a little football match or cricket match. We had hoops that would be made out of a cycle wheel or a proper one that was made, and we used to run with the hoop. When acorns were about, we made pop guns. If you cut big elderberry tree stalks, there was pith in the middle and what we used to do was push all the pith out and make it hollow so that you could see through it. Then we got a stick so that it worked up nicely and we used to tow the end, make it all bushy. We split an acorn in half and put that in the end of the barrel and put it on our chests and would then shoot out the acorn. You would be surprised at the distance that went.'

'The games we played were spinning tops and different varieties of games with marbles. One game we used to play was Egg in the Cap. We would take our hats off and lay them down by a wall and one of us would have a tennis ball, throw it into one of the hats and whoever's hat that went into, they had to get the ball and try and hit one of the other boys before he got to a place which was marked out in the road.'

'We used to have school sports on Empire Day. In the morning for what they could afford, the mothers' sent bread, margarine, bits and pieces and everyone converged on the school. All the kids and the teachers would be there and they'd put tables up and they'd make sandwiches and people would send apples, bananas and all sorts of food. It was a day from eleven o'clock in the morning that would go on until eight or nine o'clock at night. All day long, dancing the maypole and races for various age groups, a football match and a cricket match. When your father left off work at night, he'd have a wash and shave and they'd all come down to the school. That would be Empire Day, a real day out.'

Tramps

In those days, tramps wandered around the country and particularly around Norfolk. If they stayed the night at the workhouse, which is now St. Michael's Hospital, they had either to do some digging or saw chunks off old sleepers that came from one of the two stations at Aylsham. Some of them who couldn't do any sawing, had to chop the wood into small pieces for kindling and most of it went to the school which helped to lay the fires. In the morning you'd see them leave, but previous to that if they had any valuables on them, they would dig a hole in the hedge and hide them up. If they had any money or valuables on them, the workhouse would make them pay for anything they had to eat. According to them, they were penniless. The tramps would come to people's doors with a billy can and ask for hot water and people would invariably give them tea or cocoa. The tramps would sit by a hedge and have bread and cheese or whatever they were given.

You wouldn't see much of the tramps in winter, I think I'm right in saying they were allowed more than one or two nights in the workhouse, but in summer it was one night only. I can remember the workhouse master was Mr Rylands and the matron was Mrs Rylands. The police used to have a look to see what the tramps were up to because if there was a chicken handy or anything else it was a dinner for the tramps. They'd go into a field and scrape a few spuds up, but the farmers weren't too perturbed about them. Once they got a few potatoes, they'd sit on the side of the road and they'd pour water into some sort of can and have a boil up. They knew their rounds and they knew how long it took between the various workhouses scattered about.

The tramps weren't any trouble, I can't recall any of them taking drink and there weren't any alcoholics. In the summer, they would ask people who had orchards if they'd give them some apples. In some cases they'd even stop and do a bit of hedge trimming and they'd trim the hedge for some spuds, apples or bread and cheese. A lot of them would work, that was their life and they didn't want to be shut indoors. They were that type of person. There were women tramps as well as men and at the workhouse, they had to do scrubbing, washing and window cleaning and mending.'